Staying Safe

Pedestrian Safety

by Sarah L. Schuette

Consultant: Shonette Doggett, coalition coordinator
Safe Kids Greater East Metro/St. Croix Valley
St. Paul, Minnesota

PEBBLE
a capstone imprint

Little Pebble is published by Pebble
1710 Roe Crest Drive
North Mankato, Minnesota 56003
www.mycapstone.com

Library of Congress Cataloging-in-Publication Data
Names: Schuette, Sarah L., 1976– author.
Title: Pedestrian safety / by Sarah L. Schuette.
Description: North Mankato, Minnesota : Pebble,
[2020] | Series: Little pebble. staying safe! | Includes
bibliographical references and index. | Audience: Ages
6–8. | Audience: Grades K to grade 3. Identifiers: LCCN
2018052364| ISBN 9781977108722 (hardcover) | ISBN
9781977110305 (pbk.) | ISBN 9781977108807 (ebook
pdf) Subjects: LCSH: Traffic safety—Juvenile literature.
| Pedestrians—Juvenile literature. Classification: LCC
HE5614.2 .S38 2020 | DDC 363.12/5—dc23
LC record available at https://lccn.loc.gov/2018052364

Editorial Credits

Erika L. Shores, editor; Heidi Thompson, designer;
Morgan Walters, media researcher; Marcy Morin,
scheduler; Tori Abraham, production specialist

Photo Credits

All photos by Capstone Studio/Karon Dubke

All internet sites appearing in back matter were available
and accurate when this book was sent to press.

The author dedicates this book to her niece
and nephew, Muriel and Wesley Hilgers.
We like going for walks together.

Printed and bound in China.
001671

Table of Contents

Going for a Walk

We stay safe on a walk.

We walk during the day.

We only use sidewalks

or paths.

Bo keeps his head up.

He watches where

he's going.

Crossing the Street

Stop!

Wes stops three big steps from the curb.

Look!

Wes follows traffic signals.

This sign means go.

Listen!

May listens for traffic.

She looks left, then right.

She looks left again.

15

We hold hands.
We always cross
with an adult.

Ella walks quickly
in the crosswalk.
She doesn't run.

Walking Safely

We have fun on a walk.

Glossary

crosswalk—a place where pedestrians can safely cross the street, often marked on the street with painted lines

curb—the edge between a street and a sidewalk or path

safe—free from harm

sidewalk—a hard path that gives people a safe place to walk or bike away from cars and other traffic

traffic—the cars, trucks, and buses that move on a road

Read More

Buitrago, Jairo. *Walk with Me.* Toronto: Groundwood Books, 2017.

Cavell-Clarke, Steffi. *Staying Safe.* Our Values. New York: Crabtree, 2018.

Heo, Yumi. *Red Light, Green Light.* New York: Cartwheel Books, 2015.

Internet Sites

Safe Kids Worldwide: How to Walk
www.safekids.org/howtowalk/index.html

Safe Walking for Kids
www.safeny.ny.gov/kids/kidswalk.htm

Critical Thinking Questions

1. Where do you wait before crossing a street?

2. What should you do in a crosswalk?

3. Why might it be important to keep your head up while walking?

Index

24